A sisterhood connecte
waistbeads

About Me

THERE WILL BE NO LIES TOLD AT THIS TABLE

My journey started out as most Western African American young ladies. I knew I had greater accomplishments ahead of me but was also suffering from a subconscious conflict between myself and Western society. I had to overcome a shy phase, brought about by American standards of beauty and a curiousness of self. Thanks to my amazing, encouraging, selfless, and nurturing mother, Deborah Davis, this phase was very short-lived. Like most African American moms, my mother made a vow to provide her children with all the things she never had.

Not only did I go through puberty at a later stage in my life but growing up as a very dark-skinned female affected my self-esteem. It was a very confusing struggle. Also, it wasn't easy having a such a unique, raspy, and deep voice that never matched my physical frame. Despite my voice not matching the way I looked, it had always been a perfect match for enormous, vibrant, and comedic personality. As I realized the personality and characteristics within me could brighten up the darkest and deepest of caves, I allowed the insecurities to leave me for the rest of my life. My mother was my first comedic audience. She was my first example of strength as well as my first muse. My mother single-handedly pulled me out of an adolescent depression by just using her words and pure unadulterated love.

Sisterhood, in my definition, is a bond beyond words: it's a connection without chords and an experience without guidance. Sisterhood has made me the woman I am today. We live in a patriarchal society where black women are the lowest on the totem pole. So, we must learn to create a strength that supersedes the trials and tribulations of being a black woman in western society. No matter how hard life is, a sisterhood can be your crutch when you're physically, emotionally, and spiritually broken.

It's the goat for me!

I have walked this earth for 39 years and have yet to encounter anyone who talks more than my father or me. I had so many ideas and thoughts, and so much to say. What was I to do with all these thoughts that needed to be expressed? Well, my mother bought me my first diary way back in the 1980s. Now, I'll be honest: grammar and punctuation took a backseat. It was much more important to me to get the thousands of ideas of I had out. Since then, I have been an avid believer in journaling. As the saying goes; the pen is but a slave to your thoughts. Many years later and several thousand experiences later, I am still writing. Writing, to me, is the only form of expression that lacks judgement until shared with an outside audience.

My waist bead journey was never for me or about me. I was merely a vessel to promote sisterhood, culture, and love throughout the hearts and minds of other black women who needed a sisterhood they could not physically attain. If you truly believe in universal laws, then you to understand why this book is so important to Western society in today climate and current state.

Waist Beads and Western Society

BY DONNA STOREY

https://linktr.ee/anaturalhairstorey

Chapters

Chapters

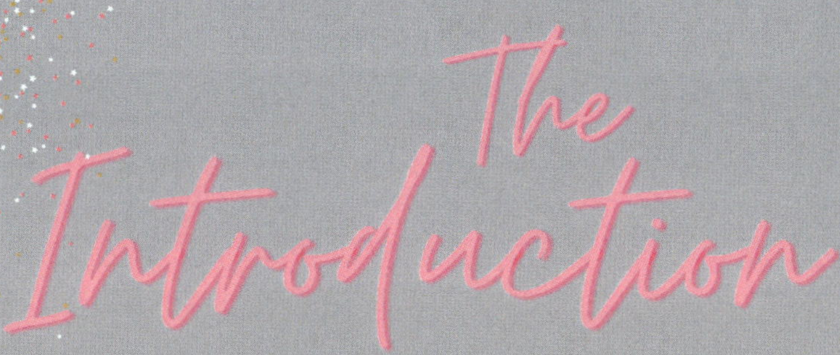

The Introduction

Western society teaches us in this world that all connections must be external; that you are alone and must learn the universe through reading, visual aids, and accumulated experiences. This could not be any further from the truth. Waist beads are a mystical, magical piece of African culture buried deep inside our mitochondrial DNA. My discovery of waist beads came at a time when I was subconsciously looking to find myself.

In 2016, like many inhabitants of the United States, I was extremely uncomfortable as an African American. My husband and I were fed up with the racial injustice and treatment of African Americans in this day and age. We made a vow to disconnect from a society that no longer served us. This was my first step into a conscious lifestyle.

One of the first things I realized is that I wanted to change my physical appearance. Even though my husband thought my body looked perfect, I thought my curvy body was disproportionate. When I looked at myself in the mirror, the reflection staring back at me screamed of childbirth, negligent eating, and a lack of physical exercise. My husband is approximately four years younger than me and one of the things that attracted him to me was my curvy silhouette. Naturally, it was a high priority for me to maintain that image for him as well as myself.

So, research became my best friend. I discovered Alfredo Bowman who is better known as Dr. Sebi. His charismatic energy immediately caught my attention. Dr. Sebi's impressive research regarding food and health encouraged me to change what I eat. Being a proactive woman means acceleration by, as brother Malcolm X said, any means necessary. So, that was it! I decided to take the necessary measures and only do things that would help me drop inches and contour my body.

Though I adopted a diet of alkaline-rich foods, I still felt like I needed more assistance to help shape my body. So, there I was ... Still at a crossroads, wondering how in the entire fuck was I going to slim down my waist without losing my womanly curves.

Now I just want to point out here really quick that if you are on a true conscious journey, when you rely on outside forces and leaders it is a sign you are not ready to ascend. Never be led: this is the first rule that should never be broken.

You see, in the world of exercise, you cannot tell your body where to lose weight. So, I relied on an outside force to transform my target area which was my got-damn waist. Even though I had seen women shaped worse than me, due to my small breasts and large bottom, having a large midsection was a no-no.

So, it was during my research that I discovered waist trainers. You must understand the waist trainer is a "bad bitch" whose job is to apply pressure until your waist is almost nonexistent. I started to wonder if there were any alternative ways to train your waist.

Why yes there was!

After a quick Google search of "alternative ways to train my waist," I found what would change my life forever. The infamous "African WAIST BEAD" ... and the rest is history.

However, before I write myself into an early grave, I've got to explain how this small, classy, inconspicuous tool for manifestation changed my mind, body, and soul. I am the type of woman that runs full speed ahead with new information, new opportunity, and a chance to better myself and I was ecstatic over my discovery of waist beads. I thought what I had discovered was merely a tool that would allow me to gauge my weight loss, but it was so much more.

In the beginning, I felt very proud to adorn my body with an African tradition that was different from Kente cloths, head wraps, and charms from the African continent. Adopting African culture was very significant to my spiritual growth because consciousness was what I ultimately longed for. Losing inches from my waist was just an added incentive.

I have read and researched this topic wonderful queens, princesses, witches, goddesses, fairies and waist bead warriors so without further ado I present to you my baby; my first but not last book,
Waist Beads and Western Society!

Oh! As a sidenote, if you know anything about Baltimore vernacular, then you understand that expressive profanity is essential in storytelling and description. (Hint: The word "fuck," believe it or not, attracted me a YouTube following of 5k in 1 year.)

Chapter One

20th Century Waist Bead Discovery

In Nigeria, it is called the *Jigida*. While in Yoruba land, which is in southern Nigeria, it is called the *Bebedi*. In southeast Nigeria, it is called *Mgbaji.* The waist bead is also known as *Ileke Idi*, *Yomba*, *Giri- Giri*, and the *Djalay*.

During this journey, I've often felt like Steve Irwin - hunting the elusive crocodile. Except in my case, it's the history of waist beads. And to be completely honest, my search was very vague. Google was the first place I decided to search. Don't get me wrong - I learned much of my information from Google; however, what is an expedition in a foreign land without consulting with the indigenous people?

Historically, when archaeologists set out explore the world, they might discover ancient artifacts covered with a foreign language. The key to understanding the history, purpose, origin, and usage of historical artifacts (such as the Rosetta Stone) is translation. So, I began looking for someone who looked like me, but was from a different land and could explain the mysteries of the African waist bead.

The only person I felt comfortable asking was an older woman who worked at my favorite lunch spot. She was always kind to me and that made it easy to build a simple relationship with her. We would have general conversations about life for the 30 minutes I was allotted for my lunch break. It took me about a month to work up the courage to ask her about waist beads. She smiled and laughed deeply when I said, "waist beads." Much to my delight, she told me she would be making a trip to Africa and could bring back some authentic African waist beads when she returned. I felt like a kid in a candy store!

Every time I laid eyes on this woman, I inquired about her travel dates. In fact, I asked about her travel plans so much that whenever she saw me, she would start our conversations off with, "Baby, I don't know when I'm going, but I promise I will let you know." Then we would both laugh about it. To be honest, though, it got to a point where I wanted to finance her trip just to get my hands on them African waist beads.

However, just as the Spirit gives, it also takes.

One day I walked into the restaurant to greet my new African mother and she was gone. In my mind, she had left for her trip and would surely return with either African waist beads or an amazing story of her family and friends. After a month of missing my friend, I mustered up the courage to ask management what happened to her. Unfortunately, I was told she had left the job about a month ago. I was devastated. Where was my new mom whose energy embraced me as soon as I walked through the door? Where could she have gone? Did she stay in Africa? Did she find a new job? Was she even real?

At the time, I felt as though the waist beads were not within my reach. However, looking back, I realize the waist beads were calling me closer and closer to my divinity. The brief relationship I developed with my African mother ignited my love and desire for my true African mother - which was the continent of Africa, the Motherland. This made me realize Pan-Africanism should be held in the highest regard.

How was it that I had no connection the Motherland despite her being the origin of my history? How was it that my ancestors would come from a land where there exist thousands upon thousands of native tongues, yet I knew not one? How was it that I felt closer to the people who looked nothing like me, but felt so distant from the people who were my spitting image?

The search was just beginning.

The impression these elusive, African waist beads made on my heart wouldn't allow me to sleep until I connected with them. Full of anticipation, excitement, and drive - I made a vow to run towards the waist beads instead of away from them. This was me subconsciously running towards my higher self. Brother Bobby Hemmit said, "the acquiring of information is the rebirth of self to intern build a new minc, ultimately building new ways of thought." My mind was most certainly under construction.

As I searched, I started to realize that in some ways waist beads had been separated from the bead culture in Africa. There were numerous articles and books about the history of the bead in Africa; however, if waist beads were mentioned, it was only a small paragraph. How could such a huge piece of matriarchal history be dismissed? How could what adorn the wombs of the ancient Kamites and birthed nations of gods who will forever be documented on pyramid walls be forgotten? One phrase can summarize this disaster: "the methodical destruction of African history," which started with the destruction of goddess worship and/or remembrance.

Well, if I must be the energy devoted to resurrecting African waist beads in Western society, I pledge my life and allegiance to thee.

Chapter Two

THE HISTORY OF WAIST BEADS

When beginning the search for yourself, you must definitely start at the roots. There is an African proverb which states, "When roots are deep, there is no reason to fear the wind." My cultural roots are firmly grounded in the African diaspora. So, I started my journey in the land of black earth, also known as Kemet and modern-day Egypt. To be completely honest, I was gently directed to Egypt by another amazing woman that I met along my journey. I discovered her in my initial search for the perfect waist bead.

After going into different, small African boutiques and trying various types of waist beads, I still felt incomplete. Every time I tried to engage in conversation with the young ladies behind the counter of these boutiques, I was given little to no information. Determined not to be discouraged, I still purchased waist beads from these boutiques and continued my journey. I initially started with stretchy waist beads which were beautiful; however, they did not teach me anything about my womb or its true history.

After literally breaking over ten pairs of waist beads, I upgraded to a waist bead which was constructed of a strong cordage and a screw clasp. I still managed to break that during my trip to Mardi Gras when I took a bathroom break after consuming more than the legal limit of intoxicants known as alcohol.

I then turned to Instagram where I attempted to use photographs posted by complete strangers in order to find the perfect waist bead. I reached out with excitement! I was either ignored or dismissed, possibly due to my numerous questions and inquisitive nature. Also, when I did reach out to African jewelry makers, the shipping cost would greatly outweigh the value of the waist bead which made it not worth purchasing.

Late one night, I stumbled upon a wonderful lady by the name of Tracy Bell-Borden. Her background was rooted in Native American history. Tracy was also a very proactive activist who stood-up for issues affecting the black community in California. I reached out to her and she responded to me in a timely manner. She educated me on several topics of consciousness and waist beads. She was the goddess that introduced me to crystals as a form of spiritual medication and actually prescribed me a cocktail of crystals to treat any issues I was having at the moment.

Once I received my first set of waist beads from Tracey, I was madly in love. These were my first set of crystal waist beads and I was infatuated! Tracy educated me on how to prepare and program them with my intentions.

In the beginning stages of my conscious journey, I wasn't experienced in spirituality. But after meeting Tracey, I became an eager and astute student. I enthusiastically jotted down her instructions and followed everything to the letter. Tracy was just as valuable as the WAIST BEADS, directing me on how to start my journey in the beginning. As mentioned earlier, she was the one who directed me to start my journey with Egypt. She recommended books like Egypt on the Potomac by Anthony Browder. She suggested I find anything I could get my hands on by C. Freeman El, Dr. Ben Yosef, and Dr. John Henrik Clarke.

I continued my journey of knowledge with laser focus. Honestly, this was a beautiful but trying time for me because I had to come to terms with the fact that I had been indoctrinated and not educated. I had been bamboozled and led astray by the same slave master who promised equality. I was almost consumed by the deception; my thoughts ran rapid and I felt compelled to be a messenger of this information to free my people.

However, I quickly learned that the conscious African American is an occult priesthood of gods and goddesses. This information will not be received or digested by those who are asleep or uninterested in spirituality. I learned quickly to reserve my light and energy for those who could receive and reciprocate.

Lastly, I learned there are levels of consciousness, delegated by levels of fear which are determined by religion - specifically Christianity. To enslave a people, you must demonize their gods and religious beliefs. Also, there is a constant assault on our evolutionary consciousness, delivered by means of inadequate food and water, limited sleep, and limited education. Regardless of how many college degrees you possess, the intelligence needed to further your consciousness does not lie in a course curriculum or university appointed prerequisite books; nor is it found in standardized tests and quizzes created by white supremacy.

There is a spiritual intellect deep in your DNA, embedded in your cellular structure, and handed down generation to generation. The greats that publicized this conscious revolution have an inner knowing. They know that intuition is the universe's true form of intelligence and it has been downloaded into each cell of our bodies. I searched for freedom inside a jail that was passed down from a slave ship named Jesus. That's right – the first slave ship to arrive in Africa was named Jesus of Lübeck.

I said to myself, "No more." No more indoctrination, no more false information, no more hidden agendas. Intuition and knowledge via my connection to the waist bead and culture will lead me.

My third and last resort to gaining historical information about waist beads was to reach out to an African born vendor that I met through months of searching relentlessly on marketing websites. I finally built up the strength and courage to ask her about the product I'd purchased from her a numerous amount of times. At this point in my life, I had purchased over 500 waist beads from this lovely, humble woman. Her product was exactly what I was searching for and priced very reasonably.

Cautiously, because of Western preconceived notions of native Africans that would possibly take my money and leave me stranded, I initially purchased a small amount of waist beads. As I explained to her how much I needed her help and how thankful I was to be in contact with her, she expressed the same gratitude. That made me comfortable in proceeding with our business arrangement and I knew she could help me further my career.

After three months of quality waist beads, shipped in a timely fashion, I decided to pop the question... and no, I'm not talking about marriage. I asked if she would be open to allowing me to interview her about waist beads and their history.

At first, she respectfully declined. But, being the saleswoman that I am, I did not take the first "no" she gave me. I automatically assumed that she did not want her personal information displayed.
I'm a firm believer in respecting one's personal privacy and boundaries. So, I posed a second question by way of general knowledge which did not divulge her information. I was very concerned because her response was not immediate. I suppose after thinking about it for a while, she finally decided to respond to my questions with general answers.

What I now understand is that waist beads are more than just jewelry. Waist beads are how cultures connect to sisterhood. The sisterhood is cloaked in secret information, rituals, and a connecting, unconditional love. What I asked of her was not just a question. What I had requested was an initiation into an ancient sisterhood. At the time, she did not know if I was worthy to join.

I patiently waited, making sure I did not make her feel uncomfortable or rushed to get the information I needed. After she delivered my waist beads, she explained that in her village, waist beads were no longer of importance. However, waist beads and other forms of jewelry had turned into a form of currency.

I explained how amazing, highly acclaimed and sought after her jewelry was. I had just completed my first photo shoot. I also mentioned the book that I was writing. You'd think these things would be impressive, but what I discovered is that Western ideals of success wasn't necessarily the same as for people in Nairobi, Kenya.

There had to be things that were much more important than documenting waist beads from an African American's point of view. This drove me even further to complete this book. This was proof that the significance of waist beads was information that needed to be told to every African American woman who was looking to connect with her history, culture, and rituals through the art of beading.

During the time I was waiting for my vendor's response, I decided I should stick to what I know and immerse myself in research. So, that's what I did. What I initially learned about waist beads was that they were a part of African wear, which started way back in the black land called Kemet – or as it is known today, Egypt. When I began trying to narrow down which Egyptian pyramids depicted waist beads, I had some trouble. I checked out several Medew Netcher hieroglyphs (the ancient language of Kemet) on pyramids such as the Temple of Dendera and the Pyramids of Giza. Still, I couldn't confirm waist beads being depicted on any of the pyramid walls.

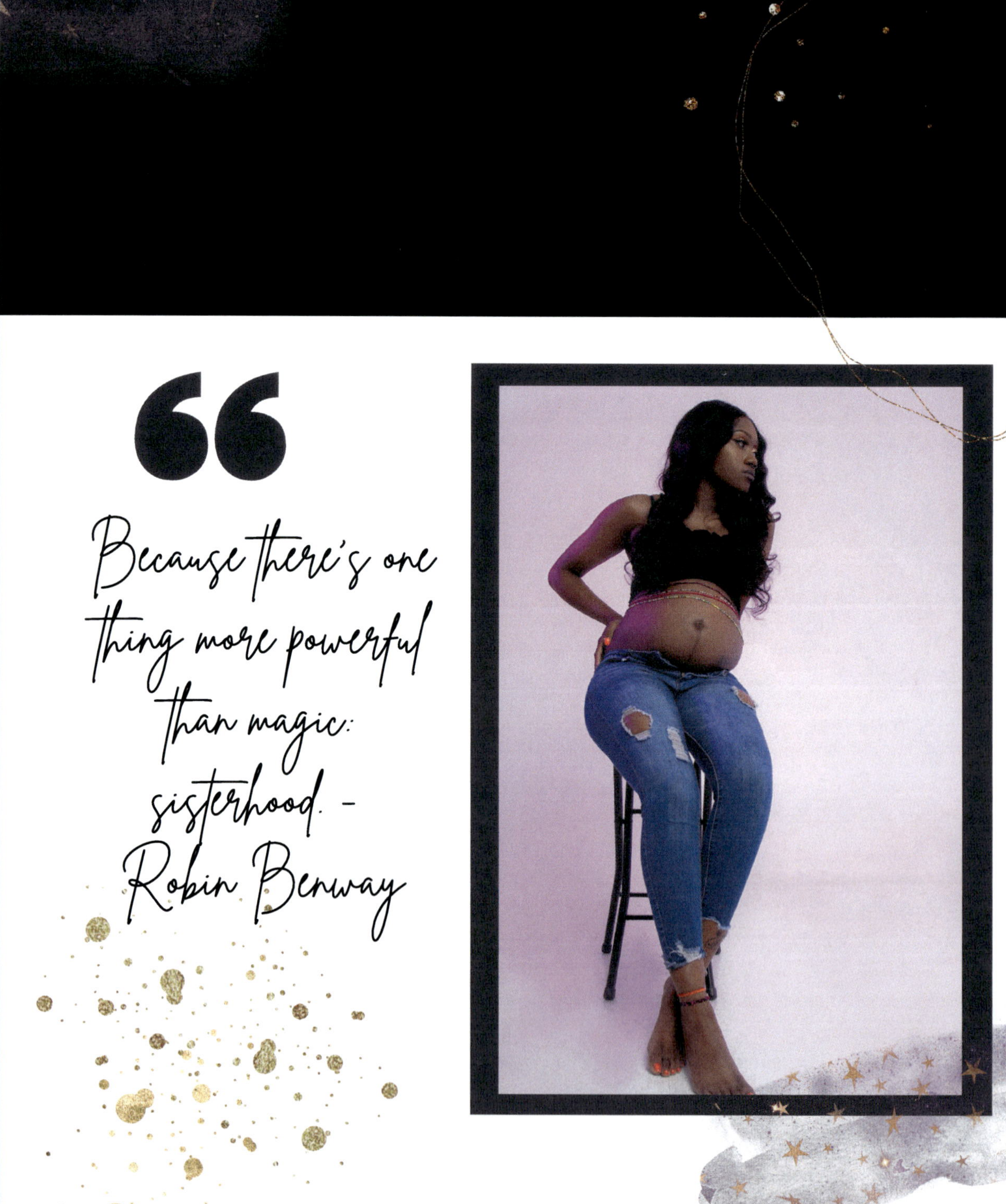
"
Because there's one thing more powerful than magic: sisterhood. - Robin Benway

However, there was a picture online of what seemed to be an Egyptian girl bringing forth offerings to a queen. In this picture, she had on waist beads. This led me to believe there were several things that could've possibly happened.

The first possibility was that there are pyramids throughout Egypt that have not been publicly displayed. The picture in question may have come from one of those. Similarly, from the Olmec Heads in Aztec, Mexico to places in America, certain pieces of our history have been hidden. I would never doubt that this picture, which was heavily circulated in the waist bead community, was incorrect. Eventually, I turned to several Egyptian history books that I purchased in order to dig deeper in hopes of finding some sort of historical documentation on waist beads being worn in Kemet.

Waist beads have different meanings for different African tribes and cultures. Initially, I learned waist beads were placed on newborn babies to gauge if they were gaining weight properly. It was used also identify their gender. You see, in some African cultures, names hold a huge significance in the child's life. After a child is born, the child's name would be given during a naming ceremony. Until then the naming ceremony was held, waist beads would identify if the child was a boy or a girl. After the naming ceremony was complete and the child was shown to be gaining weight on a consistent basis, then the waist beads would be removed from the boys. However, the little girls would continue their journey of wearing waist beads. So, it's safe to say that in some African cultures, women have worn waist beads throughout their entire lives.

Waist beads also became the first form of clothing. Certain things could be attached to waist beads to free the hands during travel and daily routine. In Ghanaian culture, waist beads were also used to carry menstrual cloths during that time of the month. Some waist beads were used as covering for sensitive areas. Some men wore rope, similar to waist beads, to cover their genitalia. Women would attach certain loose beading and material to cover their genitalia as well. As with every wonderful piece of clothing or jewelry, waist beads evolved into becoming a part of feminine culture. In some tribes, waist beads represented lingerie and became a sex symbol to the opposite sex.

I watched a few African documentaries back in 2019 that discussed how waist beads enticed men and how they can be mesmerized by them. Of course, the answers varied based on the individual's opinion. But, most of the men admitted waist beads did indeed entice them. They claimed the waist beads directed their eyes to the woman's midsection, where they could view and behold all her amazing curves. The men stated they were immediately drawn to the woman's bottom, which we all know is considered extremely attractive and alluring to men of all cultures. And since we're on the topic of bottoms, some African cultures claim that waist beads were solely responsible for giving their women a curvaceous, round bottom.

As I continued to research, my journey expanded into learning about different cultures. Some cultures used waist beads to identify certain tribal principles, characteristics, and features. This was done by changing the colors of the beads as well as adding different charms and jewels.

Waist beads were also given to girls once they began menstruation. This signified or represented a rite of passage for the child. The girl was now going from young adulthood to womanhood. The gifting of waist beads to a young girl when started her menstrual cycle was about more than the child starting her period. The waist beads were meant to aid her with the work that went into building and strengthening her physically, mentally, and spiritually so that she became a well-rounded woman.

In many cultures, this was done by making sure that the young girl was mentored by a seasoned woman who had lived a full life, which included marriage, childbirth, and hard work. This woman would groom the young girl and help her tap into her divine feminine energy so she could become a reputable woman. The little girl would be taught how to feed and care for babies. She would also be taught about feminine hygiene, how to care for a spouse, and ways of communicating with her husband and his family. The girl was instructed on how to care for her home which included cleaning, laundry, and cooking. She learned proper etiquette on caring for herself and how to properly entertain. She also learned how to love and be loyal to her husband. And most importantly, she learned everything that came along with motherhood.

Motherhood is very important. In Africa wealth is not based off monetary items but rather the lineage and size of your family. Abundance was largely defined by fertility. This is also directly related to the secrecy and intimacy that waist beads hold in a woman's life. After a young lady was gifted her waist beads at her rites of passage, the next set of meaningful waist beads she received was on her wedding day. At this time, she would remove all waist beads that had been viewed or handled by any other person. Then, she would place a set of white waist beads on her waist. These were meant to only be seen by her husband. Any other set of waist beads she obtained after she was married was only to be viewed by her husband.

In some tribes, the charms on the waist beads were known as protection to the woman's womb, spirituality, and physical body. Waist beads are heavily decorated with charms. The cowrie is a well-known stone that is used in every form of jewelry made in Africa. The shells represent fertility and is a visual representation of a woman's vagina. Placing the charm on the waist beads is said to strengthen their power, giving the woman added fertility, protection, and connection with her ancestors.

In other African cultures, waist beads are enhanced with certain adornments and powers to manifest desired results. There's a waist bead that is placed in a bag full of a secret powder that is supposed to grant a woman fertility almost immediately. Waist beads were also worn to send nonverbal communication to one's partner to inform him of any changes in the woman's body. There were bells placed upon the waist beads when the woman was ready and willing to have intercourse with her partner.

Can you imagine a husband coming home to the sound of bells and a nude African woman inviting him to enter her? Can you imagine the bells sounding off as he stroked her harder or faster? The sounds and imagery of this would be so cosmically beautiful. It would be considered art, but I digress.

When the color of the waist beads were changed, the husband knew that it was that time of the month. He would patiently wait until he could enter his wife once her period was over.

Waist beads also represented a hierarchy among members of certain villages. Certain colors would adorn the matriarch of the village. Other colors would represent adolescent girls. Other colors would represent married women and other colors would represent women who needed a husband. With nonverbal communication, signs and symbols become rooted deep down in the subconscious. This is the reason why African color charts meant so much, and it's also the reason that I decided to study Colorology.

Colorology has been used since the beginning of time in Western society as a marketing tool, but the origin was never explained. Colorology began in Egypt. The ancient Egyptians learned different hues on the color chart could promote different feelings and emotions. This was handed down to all tribes connected to Egypt.

Certain colors on certain African clothing were worn at certain times to receive or send important messages. Also, in the African religion of Ifa, each deity has their own color combination to represent them. For example, Ogun is red and black whereas Oshun is gold, white, and yellow.

Reiki, which is the practice of using healing energy, was also performed over the waist beads not only to protect, but also raise the individual's vibration as well. Every benefit of each crystal on the waist beads was amplified once placed upon the skin, and more importantly, once placed upon the womb.

The outcomes were almost magic. So, I decide to take time to learn as much as I could about crystals and any other holistic forms of medication that could enhance my melanin and give me healing properties. There is a saying in Egypt: "A day you have not learned is the day you have not lived."

I am still a student of waist bead history as well as the universe.

Chapter Three

WAIST BEAD STORIES

After researching the history of waist beads, I went searching for any dated or current stories about waist beads. Unfortunately, I found very few current stories about waist beads. The frustrating part in all this was that I knew if I could have taken a trip to Africa, I would hear numerous inspirational stories about waist beads that have been handed down.
It's very frustrating being an African American and being disconnected from your Motherland, especially when you're in search of knowledge. I knew for a fact that ultimately, one day, I would visit the Motherland and buy every damn waist bead I could get my hands on! I knew that I would collect so many stories from my Motherland – enough that I could write an entire book based on the things that I knew I'd learn from Africa regarding waist beads.

First, there were numerous stories of waist beads being an amazing way to track your weight loss and add accent crop-tops and bikinis. However, I want to get a little bit deeper.

The first story I read was a very moving one about a girl who desperately wanted to wear waist beads as a child. However, her grandmother was against it. The little girl had a friend who wore waist beads. She really wanted her own pair of waist beads. One day, her friend's mom gifted her a set of waist beads, which she immediately put on. The little girl returned home, floating on cloud nine. When the little girl's grandmother found out she had waist beads, she immediately took them off her and disciplined the child with a spanking, and then educated her on why waist beads were not for little girls.

In some African cultures, waist beads are only gifted to women who are entering into the secret union of marriage. However, they are not worn daily. Instead, the African waist beads are kept near the side of the bed and only placed on a woman when she is ready to be desired by her husband. These waist beads have certain sexual connotations that are not appropriate for little girls. In the story, the little girl was so traumatized that even as a grown woman, she still feared getting a set of waist beads.

In another story, a teenage girl wore a crop-top which showed her waist beads. She began to be noticed by the public and was called a whore and a slut. In her culture, waist beads were known as a form of lingerie. They accused the young lady of seeking male attention, even from married men. She was told to go home and immediately change her outfit.

There was also a story about a man who gifted his wife a set of waist beads. It increased her sexuality and brought a new excitement to their bedroom.

I read yet another funny story in which a little girl was gifted waist beads by her father. He told her that any gentleman who attempted to have sex with her would die if he wasn't her husband. Even though the story had scared this young girl, she still dared to kiss a boy on his cheek. Shortly thereafter, he disappeared. However, after a little investigation, she discovered the boy had moved to a different village. Prior to the girl her finding out this information, she was sure the waist beads had the power to kill a man dead if she did not follow the rules given to her by her father. Can you imagine living your life, believing you had secretly murdered someone all because of your inability to control your lust?

The language barrier was another obstacle that hindered me from discovering the real history of waist beads. I'd found several videos on the history of waist beads, but they were in the native African language. There were only a very few videos recorded in English. One video in particular that had been recorded in English featured an African woman sitting in her home, being interviewed by a Caucasian woman. The African woman explained that waist beads had been handed down from generation to generation. She felt compelled to continue the culture of her tribe. After she creates her waist beads, she goes to the market to sell them. She also explained that if her daughters or granddaughters wanted to continue this part of her culture, they would have to be taught the art of waist beads in order to keep it relevant.

I also heard a story of a married woman who forgot to take off her old waist beads during the time of her wedding. When her new husband laid eyes on her in the old waist beads, he decided to call off the wedding. He said his wife-to-be was not pure and that she did not dress properly, which would translate into her not ever being a proper wife.

There were stories about many African American women who received their first of waist beads from a healer. The healer explained certain historical facts about the waist beads, and this left these women wanting to know more about waist beads. Many women found that once they wore waist beads,they immediately felt connected to a part of their history.

African jewelry is usually created by a healer or a person of high regard in the village or tribe. It is usually made with a specific intent to help the person it is gifted too.

African culture understood spiritual and mental health were just as important as being strong and intelligent. So, there were many things done to keep a healthy state of mind.

I also watched videos of native African people getting frustrated with the materialistic ways and vanity of African Americans wearing waist beads. The videos suggested that African Americans were uneducated and wore waist beads incorrectly. It was disgusting to those who knew the real history.

Other videos touched on the spiritual aspects of waist beads. There were some that said waist beads were primarily worn to remove negative energy from the wearer's spirit and those around them. Others claimed waist beads were worn to attract certain energies such self-confidence, prosperity, longevity, fertility, love, and peace. They asserted that if waist beads are not properly hidden, they will either lose their potency and/or attract the wrong energy to the wearer.

As I mentioned earlier, there are some waist beads that are created with crystals. However, crystals can also be used to create jewelry such as rings or necklaces. I remember when I got my first set of crystals and wore them publicly. I noticed that at certain times my crystals would get very hot. After doing some research, I discovered the reason. Crystals don't just send out energy, but they also absorb energy. So, in the presence of people with ill intent, the crystals will absorb the negativity and create a blockage to protect the wearer.

I also watched a few videos by an amazing group of filmmakers where they surveyed people in Africa. These filmmakers asked men if they were still found waist beads attractive. Almost 70% of the men said that it had been ingrained into their subconscious that waist beads go hand-in-hand with sexuality. When men see a woman wearing waist beads, their eyes are automatically drawn to her bottom and her vaginal area, making her seem irresistible even if she is not very curvy or vivacious. To African men, waist beads have always been a sign of feminine sexuality.

I wondered if African American men would view waist beads in the same way. My husband, who is a man of little words, expressed his desire to see me wearing waist beads. He said he always found them sexy and, at times, would touch them. I always ask the ladies about their husband's or significant other's reaction to the waist beads they purchase from me. They all have the same response: they state their husbands and significant others loved the appearance of waist beads on their naked bodies. Could it be possible that somewhere deep down in the male DNA, there is a generational affinity for women and waist beads?

Now, I'd like to note at this point that waist beads are a staple of my life. I would never insult the culture of waist beads by viewing them as just a piece of jewelry. Learning to transform my brain started with understanding that nothing in this universe is by mistake. My knowledge of waist beads would not allow me to even make or consider waist beads just for jewelry purposes.

Chapter Four
Waist Bead Evolution

When I decided to make my first set of waist beads, it was solely for personal use. However, I was so proud of my creation that I put them on display via social media. The response was almost like the combustion of fire. People close to me came to me wanting more information about the waist beads. As I look back now at some of my first creations, I realized it was pure energy fueling those beads. I've come so far and became so skilled with the designs, energy, and techniques that I've poured into my waist beads. I'm very proud of myself.

I got my first internet sale in less than a month after I started creating waist beads. I almost left work because I was so overjoyed and could not contain myself. As I explained earlier in the book, the waist beads I was using was for gauging weight loss. Many women who had been fighting with their weight was attracted to the idea of buying a set of waist beads.

However, business is always changing, and marketing is a daily routine, so my beginnings were very frustrating. I started out posting pictures of my creations on my personal social media account. I received several likes, but my sales did not grow. I reached out to a family member who owned a boutique and got some amazing business advice from her. She advised me to place my jewelry in her boutique and create an online store to sell my products.

Approximately three months after starting my business, I was finally able to get my products placed inside a boutique. Unfortunately, my joy at being having to my waist beads being sold inside a boutique quickly turned into sadness. I wasn't able to really sell anything in that environment. I felt devastated. I had a decision to make and it was very difficult. I could no longer afford to rent space in the boutique due to lack of sales.

Once I pulled my jewelry from the boutique, I had to figure out different ways to market my waist beads. I looked into celebrities wearing waist beads in order to incite a spark in people to purchase from me; however, this didn't work. Finally, I decided to use social media as a business platform and created three business pages to drive traffic to my website. Even though my sales were consistent, they were not as rapid or abundant as I would have liked.

So, then I decided to hit the vending circuit. Now that came easy to me because I am a salesman at heart. I knew I could sell my personality and product to anyone. I was lucky enough to hook up with one of the biggest African American vending shows for my first ever vending event. At that event, I made a total of $250 for two days. I paid $50 for booth rent and $5 for gas. I had made what I thought was a serious profit back in those days.

At this vendor event, I ended up connecting with a group of businesswomen who specialized in networking. I quickly became a part of their circle. After paying membership dues, I was gifted a spot of acknowledgment where I could speak about my business and have a photo shoot done as well. It was the first time I took professional photos of my product. I was also gifted a discounted vendor rate at any of the events the women's networking group hosted. They had weekly events which were very good for meeting potential customers and expanding the visibility of my brand.

However, I quickly learned from the vending circuit was that my item is a niche market item. This means that no matter how many vendor shows I attended, there would still be people who had no clue of what waist beads were, how they worked, or their spiritual significance. While I was selling waist beads, I turned into a sort of teacher, educating everyone who was curious about my product about its history, usage, and spirituality. At this time, I did not know what the universe was doing in me; but now, looking back, it was preparing me for teaching at a larger scale.

It also taught me the resilience of being a businesswoman. As a businesswoman, you must never accept defeat. It taught me that failure is forward motion, and if you learn from your trials and tribulations, you will always grow as a business. There are certain lessons that once you learn them,
you never have to learn again because going backward is the definition of insanity

After a trip to Hawaii, I was blessed with the opportunity to take in so many forms of the beaded art that it in turn changed the look of my jewelry. I was educated by a shop owner in Maui. She explained to me that there was an island in Hawaii where only indigenous folks were allowed to go. The only form of financial income on this island was a form of jewelry making, which consisted of beads and very tiny shells that were only native to that island. I had so many questions and of course, me being the inquisitive businesswoman that I am, I fired away.

She explained that on a weekly basis, there was an indigenous person who was responsible for bringing over the jewelry that was made and selling it to local shops. After the money had been collected, this person was responsible for either taking the money to the creators of the jewelry and or purchasing items that was needed for the island. This jewelry was so intricately beautiful and inspiring. It was priced at top dollar. These beautiful pieces ranged in price from $50 all the way to $300 and they were only made of shells, twine, and clasps. Talk about inspiration! After seeing this and being educated on its history, I knew I could definitely continue to create my beautiful pieces and look at this as a serious business that would change my life and many others.

As I began using waist beads as a tool for manifestation, I decided to place the beads in a place that will give me optimal awareness of my weight gain. I placed them right along the belly button region to ensure that if I overate or under ate the beads would either tighten or roll-up. Now there were some people who believed that waist beads should be worn lower, and they were quick to reprimand me.

Although I am very respectful of religion and rituals, I also know that we are the gods who've come to Earth, and we must evolve certain historical processes to bring forth light and evolution. I've instructed every single one of my customers to begin the waist bead journey in starting near their belly button region. As the beads begin to drop, you would notice progress. It was a sign that you had, in fact, began to worship and care for your temple, as well as your womb. This technique also allowed my customers to not break their beads before they became acclimated to wearing them. I want my customers to have a positive experience, even as beginners. In the subconscious mind, first impressions create perspectives and point of views. So why not start positive?

In one of my videos, I explained that even though waist beads had been traditionally worn along the waistline, due to us being babies in consciousness and African culture, we must start at the beginning. The beginning represents a journey which will lead to wellness, literally and figuratively. As the beads begin to drop, you become closer to your goal and womb. Once the beads migrate down and lay flush against your waist and hip bones, you become an expert, which means you have successfully cared for your temple.

Now you are ready to do the real work. It begins with acknowledging that there is a woman in need of healing. Then, we delve into the vibrational patterns of crystals being placed upon your womb. Once you have been prescribed crystals, and you've properly charged and programmed them, the crystals will give you the maximum healing right at the center of your divine femininity.

I always stress that your diet and environment is more than who you're around. Your diet and environment are composed of everything you visually see, everything you pick up on intuitively, everything you inhale, everything you hear audibly, and everything you ingest. I want your diet and environmental stimuli to send you to a deeper level of consciousness and self-awareness. Once aware, you will make cleansing your energy a top priority. But these are responsibilities you cannot grasp until you have healed the temple.

Mental and emotional clutter must be detoxed. It must be removed on a regular basis to prevent the ingestion of things which will lower your vibration. It is impossible to have higher thoughts and/or vibrations if you have not properly cleansed your body of harmful toxins, self-deprecating thoughts, and negative, external stimuli.

The evolution of waist beads had become so profound to me because we were really learning all our historical downloads via DNA and research. The only obstacle is that when you don't learn from a teacher, you have more creative freedom to tailor things to fit your needs. Although, I do wish I had an African mother figure to teach me all the ways of waist beads. But, as a motherless child, I had to teach myself these lessons, which ultimately gave me freedom to explore tradition and the unknown. The interesting part was that no matter how futuristic I believed my concepts of waist beads to be, I began to realize that I had from the very beginning been in divine alignment with the Source - the Source being the intelligence stored in my DNA. It's probably more accurate to say that I was actually in divine realignment with the principles of ancient times and holistic practices. When life is viewed as a circle, it properly explains the transference of energy around and around.

Somehow, in a past life, I was a healer. I know this because not only was I healing women all over the world, but I had also been told by several mystical, intuitive women that my past was that of a healer and it had been in my DNA. The best way to describe it is that your DNA provides you with much more than looks and family resemblance. If your mitochondrial DNA provide you with curves much like our great, great, great, great grandmothers then who's to say that same DNA did not download a wealth of information that must be unlocked through conscious awareness?

Royal lineage does not start because it is not acknowledged; therefore, knowledge is the key to unlocking intelligence in your DNA. Some of our historical stories were downloaded directly into our right brain and we retain the information from the kings and queens from which we descended. The way I describe it to my children is that in the beginning, you are nothing more than a spirit, and you are born once you obtain flesh. As your flesh deteriorates, your spirit is released from its physical prison and live an everlasting life of energy and fluid motion, giving us the choice of reincarnation or life in the ancestral realm.

This is the circle of life. This is evolution: whether you born without wisdom teeth or are born a clairvoyant. Higher self is regaining knowledge of self; including but not limited to all incarnations, messages from the dream realm, and downloads received during astral travel which is internal power. Celestial intuition created gods, communities, religion, art, and warfare which encompasses the balance of life we know as alchemy.

Chapter Five.

Waist Beads for Healing

The beginning of your conscious journey starts with the unveiling of the truth. That is a prerequisite to healing the pineal gland. The mind, body, and soul are unable to heal if it's under constant trauma and turmoil. This turmoil comes when you are not given the truth while learning in your adolescence. As the mind matures, you start to solve several problems that were programmed into the subconscious as an adolescent.

According to my research, women who began to heal the temple first, which includes changing their diet and exercise regimen, were stronger in their ability to manifest wants and desires. Most women are surprised when they find out that trauma is harbored in the womb. Until you identify your trauma, which allow you to create a path to healing you are unable to have a balanced, trusting, and healthy relationship with anyone. This will hinder your relationships with your parents, your siblings, your partner, your coworkers, and most of all, yourself. Self-love is the beginning to a holistic lifestyle. Having a holistic outlook on life changes how you interact with the world, the cosmos, nature, spirituality, and the soul.

Women of African descent tend to rely on ancient processes and practices to heal themselves, whether it be hair care, skin care, or the beloved womb wellness. Since ancient times, women have been known as the creators of society and civilization. Long before Western society damaged how the world perceives women, we were viewed as goddesses because of our ability to bring forth life. This superpower has resided in our wombs since ancient times; this is how we connect to our divine feminine power.

Womb connection can also help you access and increase self-esteem, which is typically destroyed when a woman relies on current Western ideals of beauty and lifestyle. Your self-image and the overall views of yourself was taken away during slavery and the only way to reconnect with this is through self-love which has been embedded in your DNA. It is time to get back your culture. If you look on the Egyptian walls, you will notice women of all skin tones with their natural hair and their midsection out for the whole world to behold, regardless of their shapes or stature.

Processed foods that have stolen your shape and self-confidence. It's also a poison to the mind, body, and soul. We have been raised on foods that have damaged our neural systems, intestinal tract, gastric systems, and quality of life. To reclaim your authentic self, you must adjust the way you think, eat, sleep, behave, and move. Once you begin to reset the mind, the body falls in line.

Most people are surprised when they find their second brain lies in their intestinal track - most commonly known as our gut. If your gut does not have the proper nourishment, you cannot have healthy thoughts. An unhealthy gut affects your decision making, emotional state, and physical state. Women typically feel emotion in their gut or lower abdomen. When you believe a situation feels weird, you may get an uncomfortable feeling in the pit of your stomach. However, this is your intuition and your intuition is housed within the womb.

In the words of Queen Afua, "how can you have a positive relationship with anyone if you can't have one with yourself first?"

We begin with a clear line of communication to one's self. This starts with listening and interpreting sign and signals from your body. A clear line of communication can also be established by either meditating or ntalking aloud to your womb. I have learned that to fix a situation, you need to establish the when's, what's, how's, and why's. When did you start to look into the mirror and say, "I'm not happy with my image."?

The "what" is the situations that led to your insecurities. This includes negative self-images, childhood trauma, and past traumas. The "How" is a methodical plan to start self-healing. A simple plan can begin with expanding your knowledge of history and culture. This plan can also incorporate healthier eating and drinking water daily You can also start with walking, which seems very simple, but if you change these three things, you will begin to ascend spiritually.

As I mentioned earlier, when you reset the mind, the body follows. Since the dawn of time, women have been encouraged to hold their womb in the highest regard. I say let's take a page from our own history and place our womb at the very top of our healing.

We can also use the process of Reiki to change the frequency and vibration of our energy field. Different crystals placed along the chakra system produces the desired frequencies that balance and stabilize the body's energy. Reiki wisdom teaches that everything on mother earth vibrates at its own frequency. When crystals are placed upon the womb, the outcomes have been astronomical. Placing a crystal on your womb gives you all the benefits of that crystal, helping your intuition and connection self.

Sisterhood is a funny thing. It's easy to recognize, but hard to define.
– Pearl Cleage

For example, Clear Quartz is known for its ability to remove negative energy and absorb positive energy. This is exactly what it does to your womb. It creates a positive self-image and removes any negative thoughts you have harbored towards yourself. Clear Quartz is also known as an amplifier. So, once it attracts positive energy toward you, it can amplify all things positive.

Rose Quartz is known for its uncanny ability to attract love. This includes self-love. When placed upon the womb, Rose Quartz can magnify the love a woman has for herself, her body, her ideas, her goals, and her soul.

Lapis Lazuli is an ancient stone which has a unique ability to promote calm, wellness, and help women who are battling with severe past trauma.

Citrine promotes wealth and finance. Its known for its ability to promote happiness and internal joy. It's referred to as the businesswoman's stone for its ability to maintain a successful business.

Aventurine promotes prosperity, longevity, and growth. I placed a small stone of aventurine in my hair and every day, I was able to come up with different ideas for improving myself not only mentally, but in business and health as well.

When these crystals are strung upon the womb, their vibrations promote holistic, healthy healing. As the crystals become less powerful, they will need to be charged. This is done through meditation, sage, moonlight, or soil. Water is also key for curing the womb. It is a natural detox. Also, dancing - which is core centered - is a very good source of healing for the womb. For those who are unaware, twerking is an ancient African dance done on a regular basis. It promotes a solid core and strengthens pelvic floor muscles. The movements associated with the dance creates a vibration conducive for healing.

Unfortunately, Western society has appropriated twerking to reflect a negative and degrading image. Have you ever wondered why dance is always incorporated when a group of women gather? It's directly related to the ancient healing circle shared by priestesses and women in need of healing. So "twerk" my queens - make it a part of you weekly routine to allow your womb to express itself and heal with the vibrational pattern of dance. These dances are embedded in your DNA and were performed during ceremonial times to change energy, invoke spirits, to worship, and as self-expression.

To know oneself, you need to know your history.

Certain vocal vibrations have been removed from Western language. These missing vocal vibrations promoted healing. Chanting is an ancient, African art form. Vocal tones were used to promote healing and elevate thought. Create a healing mantra and place it on your wall. Repeating it daily with a melody can accelerate womb healing.

Also, your body is composed of 70% water and water is known as an absolute solvent meaning it absorbs everything internalized (negative and positive).

I created a sister circle with women from all races, religions, ages, and classes to be able to have a safe space to begin to heal. They were encouraged to vocalize their traumas in a positive, nonjudgmental environment. We try to give these women sound advice to help them along their journey. All these methods will allow you to use waist beads as a way to heal your womb.

Chapter Six
Waist Beads & Sisterhood

From long, long ago, waist beads and sisterhood have complemented each other. When the first woman created the first strand of waist beads and tied them on her waist, there was another woman there watching and observing the process. Whether that woman was her daughter, a sister, a friend, or mother, there has always been women present. The first mother who tied a strand of waist beads around her infant to gauge its weight gain showed this process to another mother who adopted this process to ensure her child grew properly. Recipes have been handed down, literally from one woman's hand to another. The women would share information and rituals that would be passed from generation to generation.

Thinking about how important this exchange of information is will allow you to put the art of beading into perspective. Before waist beads even were considered a vital piece of jewelry, they were important enough to sell for money. They were passed down from woman to woman. As you are aware, a woman's intuition supersede logic. When a woman gives you any gift, you should understand that this is coming from a place of love. Divine intuition is the nurturing of abilities, and the gift she gives is a nonverbal way of communicating that she wants you to grow and flourish.

For the last two years, I have sold waist beads to women who all were on a journey for self-betterment. These women subconsciously looked for other women who had the same thoughts, ideas, and perspectives. Knowingly and unknowingly, they also were looking for more information about an ancient art that was established long before they were even thought of.

I can never take the credit for starting the waist bead movement. There were several queens before me who were lucky enough to be related to women who came from our Motherland - Africa. I am queen who desires to empower other women through what empowered me. As I learned about the culture, I knew it was my mission to find a platform to distribute the information to the masses. YouTube was my opportunity to convey my message.

African American women have not been taught to view their sister as their ally, but as their adversary. I thank all the ancestors who gave me the ability to be relatable and the ability to convey love and care to my sisters. My approach on YouTube was not to be the most glamorous or the most polished. My approach was to be honest and allow people to live in their truth because I am my unapologetic, authentic self, living through my waist bead journey.

There's a familiar saying that goes "Your vibe attracts your tribe." I created content that would appeal to women of all ages, classes, creeds, and religions. I wanted to provide relevant, thought provoking, and genuine information about waist beads in an interesting and relatable way. As I spoke to these women, I soon realized that it wasn't about the information, but more about the value of healing had on their lives. I quickly became everyone's mother, big sister, best friend, or coworker. The love I received from these women was the fuel that drove me to continue my research of waist beads, sisterhood, and healing. Before I even created my monthly classes, business cruises, and social media groups, these women had already given me permission to become a part of their lives.

Sisterhood is a complex exchange of knowledge, experience, emotion, and admiration, which does not happen overnight. Trust must be earned by giving bits of yourself as well as ample time for the bits of information to be mentally digested and verified. We are living in an age where anything can be cross-referenced by Google.

I'm pleased to say – no; rather, I am honored to say that these women have inspired me to provide quality information. The one thing I learned about the sister circle is that it is a 24-hour commitment. You must be interactive. My business has always been 24 hours with an emphasis on an open-door policy. Not only am I here to help with healing, but I am also here to be a shoulder to cry on, a life coach, an accountability partner, and friend. I have developed some of the most meaningful friendships just based on our common love of waist beads. To be honest, the friendships, or rather sisters, I have gained based off waist beads are so cosmically deep that I cannot define it with words.

Sisterhood allows you to release emotions and thoughts that only another woman would understand. I make it a point to teach not only my daughters, but the younger women around me that your sister is a resource and not a parasitic being or your competition. The basic definition of sisterhood is a relationship between sisters, but what defines an actual sister? Is it blood relation? Is it a genetic precursor? Or is it a combination of events that both parties can relate to? Are sisterhood experiences only shared by certain women?

People of color were moved around to different plantations in different states to genetically engineer the perfect slave, making identifying genetic markers and characteristics very difficult. Have you ever been at an event, either at a work event or out in public, and met another

"

Sweet, crazy conversations full of half sentences, daydreams and misunderstandings more thrilling than understanding could ever be."

– Toni Morrison

woman who had a few physical similarities (such as nose, bone structure, or lips) as you? Maybe her voice sounded like you or one of your close relatives? Perhaps she completed your sentences?

These things are no coincidence. People used last names to track relatives, but because our names were changed throughout the transatlantic slave trade, there is really no way to know who is, in fact, your sister. DNA testing has evolved, and we are able to figure out what places in Africa we all originated from. But what do you do with the information after you figure out where you're from?

You must take it upon yourself to ask other sisters where they're from. Scientifically, if you share a percentage of Nigerian, Cameroon, Irish, Native American DNA with another woman that you don't know, you two could possibly be relatives! Also, familiar spirits gravitate toward familiar spirits. Sometimes, conversations go on for hours and allow you to let down your guard and share personal information with a stranger. This is not by accident. The universe has a bigger plan and makes no mistakes.

Being able to accept another woman as your sister is a great honor that should be held in the highest regard. To honor your ancestors and your culture, public displays of aggression towards one sister should be null and void. I'm saying this from a place of violence that had to be removed from my lifestyle.

As I grew and matured, I realized that violence against someone who looks like you is a self-destructive behavior, and it is exactly what Western society would like. Being conscious means that you understand that any aggressive behavior towards someone who looks like you mean that you have much more emotional growing to do. Sisters are very important in taking you to the next steps of your consciousness, whether it be learning from a Native American sister who can give you herbal information, an African sister who can give you some insight on tradition, or an older sister who can give you information about marriage and maturing in age. I am a new grandmother and older women warned me that the love you have for your grandchild is unmatched. Until I became an actual grandmother, I did not understand what they were saying.

Now, I am appreciative of the information that was given to me because I am a firm believer you must be around people exhibiting things that you would like to exhibit in order to grow. If you would like to be a great girlfriend, you must first be around the company of women who are great girlfriends. If you would like to be a great mother, you must first be around great mothers. If you would like to be a great friend, you must first be around women who take sisterhood seriously.

The best part of cultivating sisterhood is there's always another woman watching. Whether it be a daughter, a niece, or a mentee, they can continue the sister circle through watching and imitating.

I believe there is no coincidence in the fact that waist beads are placed in a circular shape around the waist and sisterhood is also known as a sister circle. Waist beads say a lot about a person, without verbally expressing one word. If you're ever at a grocery store or a beach and can observe someone else's waist beads, you will learn much about that queen based solely on her waist beads. You can gather that she is aware of some type of African culture and that she is on a self-care and betterment journey.

Sisterhood was the beginning of waist beads, the structure of waist beads, and the continuance of waist beads. If you are considering wearing waist beads or making waist beads, please continue to further this ancient art form. Emphasize that these beads are much more than "just jewelry."

Waist beads are womb wellness in its physical manifestation. Never forget that waist beads are the beginning of sisterhood, the adhesiveness of sisterhood, and the strength that connect and binds sisterhood.

As the sisterhood circle I created evolved, layers upon layers of traditions, rituals, holistic practices, and healing manifested itself. I immediately understood the only environment that was conducive enough to facilitate this experience was a safe, loving, and nonjudgmental environment. The women in a sister circle are like flowers, and when flowers are planted in the most optimum conditions, it will blossom to its fullest potential.

Chapter Seven
Waist Measurement Challenge

The Waist Measurement Challenge was a lifestyle change that a few family members and I created in order to have a blueprint to allow the waist beads to change your life. As soon as I got my first set of waist beads, I decided to go on a health kick to drop my waist beads. This included going from a plant-based diet to vegetarianism. In the waist bead community, dropping waist beads is a sign of celebration. It means that you have altered your mind and body in a positive light to shed excess weight around your midsection.

My initial goal was to become a vegetarian, eliminate processed foods from my diet, and make water a staple beverage daily. I noticed that this allowed me to maintain a weight I was comfortable with. A lot of queens don't know that your weight and diet control all aspects of everyday life such as mood, decision making, and self-confidence. Once I realized I had the keys to success, I allowed the waist beads to become a reliable means of gauging my weight. I almost did away with the scale completely.

The next step was to incorporate other like-minded, spiritual women to engage in this bi-monthly self-improvement journey. We measured our waist on the first day of the month, once again in the middle of the month, and at the very end of the month. Measurements are submitted privately and very discreetly in a direct message to me. The queen who loses the most inches from their waist are rewarded by public acknowledgement via social media. She also gains the ability to become an inspiration and beacon of light to other queens and receives a box full of spiritual items to help continue her introspective journey of enlightenment.

Over the months, the challenge evolved into a movement which helped women learn and implement healthy lifestyle changes through ancient holistic practices. I stress the word practice because it's a daily change of life. It started with a group of 15 queens and quickly grew to over 40 women, who were able to chat weekly about topics that concerned them.

This allowed the ladies to grow together as a unit. The Waist Measurement Challenge is an affordable, safe space of like-minded queens. Not only was I helping with their health, but I was building positive sisterhood interactions. It got to a point where the women who were joining didn't need health advice anymore, but they came for the camaraderie – the community of sisters who shared their deepest, darkest secrets, career goals, love advice, parenting advice, and beauty tips. Most of them had an ongoing dialogue about spirituality.

These challenges became so successful that other waist beaders decided to adopt the Waist Bead Challenge. Initially, I was very frustrated because some jewelry makers duplicated and replicated every single piece of my challenge, without even acknowledging me as the originator. However, my higher self realized this is an ancient practice that must be shared and handed down from generation to generation. I had become an agent of change and evolution. It warmed my spirit to know I was a catalyst of change. There's a saying that goes "be very careful how you create your success because it could become the universal system of success." This means each day I reevaluate and fine-tune my message to ensure I honor my ancestors and further the black evolution.

At heart, I am a Pan-Africanist who knows how sisterhood, mental, and physical health molds our society. The Waist Measurement Challenge documents your evolution by way of pictures, new topics, and new services. This promises an interactive experience every challenge. This challenge has also allowed me to keep the awareness of waist beads on the forefront of many people's mind by using social media platforms across the board on Wednesday.

Wednesday is now recognized as the day to pay respects to the waist bead community and has been designated as a day to make waist beads the topic of discussion. In 2020, I deemed myself the waist bead revolutionist to push women wellness by any means necessary. I intend to take waist beads to another level for the world to see and reestablish goddess remembrance.

My Waist Measurement Challenge is held every other month. Anyone reading this book is more than welcome to join - new people, new energies, and ideologies keep it fresh and new. There are so many levels of support for the challenge behind the scenes. There are silent supporters who don't necessarily want to become a part of a large group, but they want to support the mission. Some of the queens donate, others support my YouTube channel by liking, subscribing, and sharing my videos.

I greatly appreciate every kind word I have received. Some silent supporters begin by removing processed foods from the diet, incorporate more water, more exercise, and a monthly fast to reset the body. My Waist Measurement Challenge will always be my baby, and as a child grows, you realize your job as a parent is not to impose your views and beliefs; but rather, to support, nourish, and love the child. You also realize that it's a part of your job to create an environment that allows him or her to become their authentic and unapologetic self. My challenge has made its way around the world. I couldn't be prouder.

I want to stress it was sisterhood that allowed me to grow! Without sisterhood, I could not have made it through my darkest moments or highest successes without sisterhood!

Chapter Eight
What Do My Waist Beads Mean?

Colors have long since been an ancient way to express intentions, emotions, status, and manifest reality. When I started out on this road of becoming a healer, a Native American queen told me, “You must understand, inner stand, and over stand what you are providing to women in need of healing.” She stressed that it was imperative I educate myself on crystals and colors to aid in healing. This divine goddess also stressed how important it was to embark on my own research journey. She provided me with only tips and never any actual teaching.

As I did more research about the indigenous people of America, I learned the importance of self-discovery and rites of passages. Rites of passages identify the level of readiness; it also defines a clear line between the leaders and followers. Upon my journey, I made it a point to only study authentic African and melanated history to bring ancient practices to my Western world.

I stumbled across colorology during my research. Once I had clearly identified the foundational blocks of colorology, I realized how it was being used to market to the masses.

Listed below is a very general description of colors and what emotions they help manifest:

- Purple- African Color of Royalty
- Maroon- Moorish Staple of beauty
- White- Pureness, Cleansing, Festivals
- Black- Spirit growth, Maturity, Rites of passage
- Red- Symbolizes blood
- Blue- Peace, Togetherness, Harmony
- Silver- Symbolizes the moon
- Gold- Royalty, Wealth, Prosperity
- Yellow- High worth, Monetary wealth
- Green- Fertility, Agriculture, Land, Renewal, Growth

Crystals are also an ancient form of healing first used by the ancient Kemetic people. Several pyramids were built on crystal foundation or with crystal tips to produce the desired energy, mind state, or mood while inside of it. Crystals were also used to adorn our ancestors’ crowns, armor, ceremonial jewelry, and daily wear. Crystals were also used in magic works. Western society have long since used crystals to amplify technological advances.

When I embarked on my knowledge of these ancient stones, I decided to first understand how they were used by indigenous people. This would allow me to properly prescribe or recommend the proper way to use the power the crystals harnessed.

To my surprise, all matter has an aura or energy field based off their vibration. Stones like lava and tiger's eye were given to ancient warriors going into battle to promote courage, bravery, and protection. Green stones were used to represent the heart and promote a prosperous afterlife. Jade, which was adopted by the ancient Chinese culture, symbolizes luck, immortality, longevity, and prosperity. Historically, it was used in rituals. Also never forget, the first ancient Chinese Monks were black people with coiled hair.

The ancient Grecian, also known as the Greeks, used amethyst for hangovers and used crushed hematite to cover their soldiers and make them invisible. In Kemet, priest and pharaohs used cylinders of clear quartz to balance the body's energy.

I choose to honor my ancestors by gifting and receiving crystals to encourage healing and protection. Delving into the work of crystals require a complete transformation of your view on earthly stones because although they are inanimate, they are none the less alive. In my opinion, you must care for them by always exchanging energy and never just taking energy. Therefore, you must clean your crystals and recharge them to create a healthy relationship with them.

Pertaining to the world of waist beads, the same rules apply. Any crystals put upon your womb via waist beads will deliver energies to your womb. You must learn which crystals need to be charged by the moon or given a general Himalayan salt bath. Your crystals might need to reconnect with the earth or be smudged with sage.

These crystal regiments can also be a form of meditation and time used to connect with your higher self. I have experienced crystals communicating with others and myself by changing color as well as changing temperatures when exposed to different energies and frequencies. Crystals have been known to mysteriously disappear or reappear once they have served their purpose or are re-summoned mentally. If you're ever lucky enough to cross paths with a crystal outside of purchasing from a shop, you should be ecstatic because it's the universe obliging you with a subconscious request you made for healing.

If you are inspired to create some beautiful pieces to adorn your waist or share with others, here are a few tips:

- Get a basic knowledge of African history
- Establish a spiritually clean area to create in
- Spiritually cleanse your body and aura by meditation, ritual, or prayer
- Never create when your spiritual frequency is low
- Always sage or palo santo beads before wearing or sharing

Chapter Nine
Womb Wellness

Waist beads, for some women, are the first time they even know their exact measurements, let alone pay attention to their womb. So many women have gone years without even understanding the power they harness right below their bellybuttons. After beginning my spiritual journey, I realized that to release the built-up past trauma, I needed to do an overall spiritual cleansing of my womb. Women's intuition has been talked about from the beginning of time, but no one has ever decided to understand or examine where this intuition comes from... or even where this intuitive space is held in the body. Most women should begin with a womb cleanse and then work their way up the chakra system to the pineal gland, which is also known as the Third Eye Chakra.

Building or mending a relationship with anything starts with intentional conversation. This also holds true for releasing built-up trauma in the womb. Ask yourself when was the last time you sat down in front of a mirror or in a circle of women you could trust and talked about your traumatic experiences connected with your womb? Most women I ask say never. They are also unaware of how these traumatic experiences affect them on a daily basis.

When was the last time you verbally expressed your sorrow for a miscarriage you experienced? When was the last time you expressed your frustration or feelings of inadequacy for due to infertility? When was the last time you expressed your anxiety over the pain associated with menstruation? When was the last time you spoke about the side effects of your hysterectomy? How often do you speak of the side effects of your birth control? When was the last time you didn't have to hide the tears that flowed before, after, and during your menstrual cycle? Have you ever verbally expressed your desire for more children, and the regret of not being able to bear more children due to tubal ligation or lack of life partner? Have you been to therapy sessions to verbally unpack a rape you've endured?

Most women have not, and unfortunately, some live their entire lives without healing and suffer in silence. Most women don't know that these traumatic experiences are stored in their wombs and affect their daily existence behind the scenes.

After reading a book called *Dragon Times*, I learned that every menstrual cycle produces a different aura or frequency. A woman holds this aura or frequency until she is completely finished with menstruation. It was also said that the energy a woman produces while on her period is strong enough to alter different scientific experiments. Therefore, women who work in some very sensitive, scientific areas are encouraged to stay home and have a self-care day during her cycle.

After reading Queen Afua's *Sacred Woman*, I became aware of how important it is to address emotional, physical, and psychological issues throughout the month as opposed to internalizing it and allowing it to become trauma harbored in my womb.

The most important relationship you'll ever have in your life is the relationship with self. Learning how your organs work and how food affects the body and its vibrational frequency (both positively and negatively) is your responsibility. This responsibility falls on you because no one in the world knows what you truly desire or dislike.

We need to alter our views of food because everything we put in our mouths affects our health and emotions almost immediately. In the African American community, if you eat food that immediately makes you sleepy, it's considered a good, hardy meal. However, food that causes any type of lethargic behavior is too heavy.

Also, dairy is an enemy to the body. Once consumed, it causes the body to produce mucus. Mucus, when stored in different areas of the body, creates disease. For women especially, dairy is directly related to uterine fibroids, tumors, and cancer.

In the great words of Ifa Ase, a powerful goddess who helped me tremendously in the beginning of my conscious journey, "Water is the only drink suitable for human consumption." This statement stuck with me because we are the only animal on the planet that drinks anything other than water.

Learning about herbs and superfoods to cleanse the body, promote healthy cell growth, and build your immune system are key in womb wellness. In Western society, we don't relate sickness to what is consumed, and this is a huge part of not being able to correct these issues.

Listed below are a few food and herbs to heal your womb:

- Red raspberry leaf tea
- Milk thistle
- Dandelion root
- Ginger root
- Sea Moss
- Soursop leaves

- Vitamin C
- Kale
- Burdock Root
- Fenugreek
- Moringa
- Flaxseed
- Turmeric
- Damiana
- Baobab powder
- French thyme
- Rosemary
- Seaweed
- Coconut
- Alkaline rich water & food

Emotional healing and shedding layers of trauma is a very important part of womb wellness. I recommend finding a few women you can trust and learn from and build a sister circle. I also recommend speaking to and setting intentions for your womb. Speak aloud all the things you see for yourself like self-love, protection, a healthy womb, weight loss, success, and peace!

Proclaim it! Decree it! Declare it!

Once you speak it, exhibit supporting action. Your womb is where your intuition lies, which is why people say they have a gut feeling. Make sure you're treating your temple of divine feminine energy with the utmost respect. From personal experience, I know the better you feed the body, the better decisions you make. Your thoughts become clearer and your mood is improved.

Even depression can be related to a poor diet. You can combat some forms of depression just by getting more sunlight, walking barefoot in the grass, sitting by running water, and adding Vitamin C enriched vegetables or fruit to your diet (lemons, moringa, baobab, grapefruit). Start saying no to cow's milk and yes to almond or coconut milk. Eating non-dairy ice cream is a great start. Replacing sugary snacks with trail mix or fruit is another way to incorporate healthy eating into your diet.

Your womb is the beginning to consciousness. Please make her priority.

Chapter Ten
The Sacred Bead

Historically, beads were a form of currency that started in our motherland of Africa. Along with being used as currency, beads were also used to adorn the body. Regardless of what the beads were made from - whether it was wood, bone, glass, or shells - its worth surpassed the material used to create it.

Certain beads were worth more than others. Certain beads symbolized wealth while others symbolized lineage. Beads, as well as the art of designing jewelry, was handed down through generations making beads an interwoven part of our culture.

It has never been pinpointed or documented exactly where in Africa waist beads began. There are several pictures on the temples walls of Kemet of women wearing waist beads. This is where I assume waist beads started. Known by many different names, waist beads are credited to manifesting wealth, healing, love, success, and protection. I have been called a healer by many queens because of my commitment to women's wellness and health. However, I am a direct reflection or manifestation of everything waist beads have been known for since the dawn of time.

They have brought forth wealth in the way of knowledge and monetary gains. They have brought forth healing I never could have imagined. Waist beads have urged me to not only love myself for the cosmic goddess I am, but to spread a message of love that has touched almost every continent.

Success was just the tip of the iceberg when I meditated. My ancestors told me that beads were a part of my DNA. It was so much deeper than my passion - it became my purpose. It was me being reconnected to my Akashic records. I've always been in touch with my spirit and past lives.
The protection provided by these beads have been astounding.

As you ascend on this spiritual journey and come to the realization that you are the god of your universe, you learn that protection comes in the form of not only heightened intuition, but also the ability to listen without question. My journey has given me the ability to accept everything the universe brings forth whether it be good, bad, or indifferent. This is because my divine purpose is not in short-lived, emotional gain. It is in inner wisdom, and every single experience is leading me to higher self. Protection also comes in the form of making sound and educated decisions to guide you along your path.

It would be disrespectful for me not to mention that I got here by standing on the shoulders of my

ancestors. I would dishonor my lineage by not proclaiming that in the year 2020 I still don't fully understand the power of the sacred bead. I am forever grateful and will continue to be a muse for my culture, spreading the message of love, light, and the ability to heal thyself.

Thank You

This book is dedicated to all the queens who inspired me:

Deborah Davis, Diana Davis, DyrasheBattle, Diana Steward, Aliyah Lawson, Kennedy Storey, Seqoyah Storey, Zaiden Bowles, Aarika Newman, Tia McKintirre, Mia Lowery, Constance Storey, Ife Ase, Lisa's Fragrances, Kim Tatarsky,Shanea Leslie, Dalila Skipwith, Queen Afua, Kameysha Harris, Carmen Hollingsworth, Elisabeth Kesseah, Ya Leuisha, Nena Simon, Nefer Phoenix, Bare Lady Bontanicals, Diedra Hill, Latoria Lewis, and all the beautiful sisters of the Waist Beads Measurement Challenge.

Is solace anywhere more comforting than that in the arms of a sister? - Alice Walker

Made in the USA
Middletown, DE
19 March 2024